Orchids

Cover photograph:
Cattleya Crystal Orb 'Thwaite Grange',
a fine example of the breeder's art

Overleaf: *Angulocaste* Olympus 'Honey'
AM RHS, a superb bigeneric hybrid for
the intermediate house

Orchids

A Wisley handbook

Alec Bristow

 Cassell

The Royal Horticultural Society

Cassell Educational Limited
Artillery House, Artillery Row
London SW1P 1RT
for the Royal Horticultural Society

First published 1982
New edition, fully revised and reset 1985
Second impression, revised, 1987
Third impression 1988
British Library Cataloguing in Publication Data
Bristow, Alec
  Orchids
  1. Orchid culture
  1. Title
  635.9'3415   SB409

ISBN 0-304-31097-2

Line drawings by Alec Bristow
Photographs by Alec Bristow and Michael Warren

Typeset by Georgia Origination Ltd., Formby
Printed in Hong Kong by Wing King Tong Co. Ltd

Contents

Introduction	7
What is an orchid?	11
The orchid flower	12
The fruit and seeds	16
Start in life, natural and artificial	16
How orchids grow	18
Terrestrial orchids	18
Epiphytes and lithophytes; Sympodial growth	19
Monopodial growth	20
The inflorescence	21
The cultivation of orchids	23
Choosing your first plants	23
Greenhouses	24
Temperature: Cool house	27
Intermediate house	28
Hot house	29
Heating methods	31
Humidity	34
Light; Shading	36
Ventilation	37
Composts	38
Repotting; Watering	39
Resting; Feeding	41
Propagation	42
The most popular orchids	44
Cymbidiums	44
Paphiopedilums; Cattleyas	45
Odontoglossums	48
Dendrobiums	49
Species	50
Hardy and half-hardy orchids	51
Bletilla	52
Pleione	53
Growing orchids indoors	55
Pests and diseases	57
The naming of orchids	61
Further reading and orchid societies	64

Above: *Cymbidium* San Francisco 'Mona Lisa', which received an Award of Merit in 1978
Below: *Paphiopedilum* Diaboth 'Stonehurst', an example of the ever-popular slipper orchids

Introduction

Probably there are more legends, misconceptions and false beliefs about orchids than about any other family of flowering plants.

Such is the atmosphere of magic and mystery surrounding them that large numbers of excellent gardeners, who grow other things with triumphant success, are scared to try their hand at orchid-growing. To a large extent it is the glamour attached to the very word orchid, the association with a world of sophistication and wealth, that has been responsible for the reputation orchids have acquired of being not only beyond the dreams (and the pockets) of ordinary down-to-earth gardeners but also in some way not quite wholesome – thrilling, beautiful and alluring, but a shade wicked.

Perhaps the best way to dispel at least some of this atmosphere of mystery and high living, tinged with evil, and to show that quite normal people can grow and enjoy orchids without damage to their finances or their morals, and indeed with considerable enrichment to their lives, would be to deal with the questions most frequently asked by the public at flower shows where a display of orchids is being staged.

To start with some of the wilder – though commonly held – misconceptions, many questioners are convinced that orchids are dangerous. A frequent question is 'Where are the flesh-eating ones then?' The reason for this persistent, and quite erroneous, belief in carnivorous orchids is probably that many species do in fact trap insects, but that is not to eat them but to use them as pollinators.

Another widespread, and equally false, belief is that orchids are parasites. Although many live on trees, there are no parasitic orchids: they use the tree for support, not for nourishment.

'But they're poisonous, aren't they?' is another frequent question. Once again the answer is no; indeed, the pods of the orchid *Vanilla* have long been used as one of the most important flavourings for ice-cream and many other foodstuffs. Where the notion of poison came from is not clear, possibly from the general feeling of rather exciting evil which, as we have seen, many people have about orchids.

When all those questions based on false beliefs have been answered, there still remain many people who feel, despite their success with other kinds of flower, that orchids are somehow not for them. The feeling was put in the following words by a woman who had stood gazing in admiration and awe at a gold medal display at Chelsea Flower Show: 'I suppose they're the most seductive flowers of all, but I don't think somehow they're for me. I'm afraid I should never be able to live up to them'. She probably did not realise how exact her choice of the word 'seductive' was.

In a very literal way orchids are highly skilled in the art of seduction: the colours, markings, forms and scents of their flowers are specially developed to appeal to particular creatures on which they rely for pollination and which find them irresistible. Such creatures include many kinds of bees and wasps; in certain cases flies, beetles and other more primitive insects have been seen visiting the flowers of some species; and there are orchids highly adapted to the tastes of quite different kinds of pollinators: moths, butterflies, even birds (mainly the tiny humming-birds).

Fortunately for human orchid-lovers, it seems that the floral shapes and patterns and scents that appeal to this great variety of animal visitors appeal to them too; the only exception is the revolting stench of putrid meat which certain species of orchid give off in order to attract carrion-flies, which find the smell quite delicious. The reward the flowers get from the visitors is fertilisation. The reward the visitors get from the flowers is usually a drink of honey-sweet nectar. However, there are some orchids (including many belonging to the genus *Ophrys*) which go beyond simple seduction and which have developed remarkable powers of mimicry and deceit. Their visitors get no reward at all, only frustration.

The victims of their deception are various bees, wasps and flies, always of the male sex. What draws them to the flower is its striking resemblance to an attractive female of their own species. Not only does its mimicry appeal to the victim's sense of sight, but also to its senses of smell and touch; the flower gives off the characteristic scent with which the female insect lures a mate, and the hairs on its surface feel just like the female's soft, furry body. The male, believing he has found a partner, attempts to mate with the flower. Before he realises his mistake the flower sticks a mass of pollen to him with a kind of quick-setting glue, and he carries this with him to the next seductive flower of the same species to attract his attention, so bringing about fertilisation.

Perhaps because garbled versions of this remarkable story have got around among the gardening public, another misconception has arisen. 'Don't orchids need fertilising to make them flower?' enquirers sometimes ask. If by that they mean do the plants need feeding, the answer is most likely yes; but if they mean do they need pollinating, the answer is emphatically no. Commercial growers, who rely upon orchids for their living, go to great lengths, by the use of gauze screens and the like, to exclude bees and other pollinating insects from their glasshouses, because they know that once fertilised a flower will quickly fade; its purpose in life having been fulfilled, it no longer has any interest in preserving its good looks but turns its whole attention instead to the production of offspring. So if you want to keep your flowers looking attractive and beautiful as long as possible you must prevent them from getting fertilised. Then you will find that the blooms of many of the most popular orchids outlast those of most other plant families, remaining fresh and unblemished, either on the plant or as cut flowers in a vase, for weeks or even months.

Dendrobium infundibulum, an easily grown species from the second largest genus in the orchid family

Odontoglossum harryanum, like other members of the genus, is a reliable plant for the cool house

With some of the commonest misconceptions about orchids now cleared up, we can turn our attention to the questions most frequently asked by those whose interest has been aroused sufficiently for them to feel like trying an orchid or two but who would like a little more information, guidance, and perhaps reassurance, before they finally decide to take the plunge.

—*What exactly is an orchid?*
—*Do you have to be a millionaire to grow them?*
—*Could I grow them in my small greenhouse?*
—*How much heat do they need?*
—*Can any of them be grown in an unheated greenhouse?*
—*Will they grow indoors?*
—*Will they grow outdoors?*
—*How about pests and diseases?*
—*What do the names mean?*

Answers to all these questions will be found in the following pages.

What is an orchid?

The idea that orchids are rare and confined to the tropics is very far from true. In fact the family to which they belong – known to botanists as the Orchidaceae – is one of the largest of all families of flowering plants, and representatives can be found growing wild in nearly every part of the world, from the Arctic almost to the Antarctic and from sea level to mountainous regions thousands of metres high. Some species manage not only to survive but to thrive in places covered in snow and ice for a large part of the year. Some face such inhospitable conditions above the ground that they spend the whole of their life beneath the surface, where they grow, flower, reproduce and finally die in the dark.

Orchids vary in height from some that are several times taller than a man to others that would fit into a thimble with room to spare. Some have large, luxuriant foliage, and some have no leaves at all. Shapes, both of plants and of flowers, vary just as widely as sizes. Almost every shade of colour is to be found except jet black.

Vanda Rothschildiana, one of the most beautiful hot-house orchids

The number of orchid species in the world is estimated by some experts to be at least 25,000; others suggest that the figure may be as high as 30,000. Nobody knows for sure, since there must be many more undiscovered species in areas not fully explored by orchid specialists.

In addition to all the species, more than 60,000 artificial hybrids have been created since that day in 1856 – the most important date in the history of orchid breeding – when the first successful cross to be made by man came into flower. The number of artificial hybrids is increasing substantially all the time; the Royal Horticultural Society, as International Authority for the Registration of Orchid Hybrids, receives as many as 175 applications a month to register the name and parentage of new crosses.

Though the most spectacular orchids (or in the case of hybrids their parents), with the dazzling flowers that cause the loudest gasps of admiration at shows, do tend to have originated in the warmer parts of the world, there are many attractive kinds which are native to cooler regions. In the British Isles alone, according to the standard floras, no fewer than fifty-three different species have been recorded, plus ten or more sub-species and varieties.

With such a multitude of different kinds, widely dissimilar in appearance and habit of growth, what is it that makes an orchid an orchid? The answer is the flower, which is quite unlike that of any other family of plants.

THE ORCHID FLOWER

Perhaps the best way to demonstrate the special features of the orchid flower is to compare it with what might be called a 'normal' flower – that is, the sort of flower that more often than not is to be found in other families of plants. This 'normal' flower is essentially rather a simple affair, made up of separate and easily identifiable parts. At the base of the flower, where it joins the stalk (called the *pedicel*), is a whorl of inconspicuous organs like small leaves (the *sepals*), which before the flower opened formed the outside of the bud. Arising from inside those sepals is the most conspicuous part of the blossom, the *petals*, which are usually brightly coloured and serve to attract the attention of insects or other pollinating creatures. At the centre of the petals come the sexual parts: first the male organs, the *stamens*, consisting of thread-like *filaments* terminating in *anthers*, which burst open when they are ripe to release quantities of fine, powdery *pollen*, and inside them the female organs constituting the *pistil*, made up of the *ovary*, topped by a stalk called the *style*, crowned by the *stigma*, the surface of which when sexually receptive becomes sticky, and so able to catch the pollen grains, which adhere to it as the first step in the process of fertilisation.

The orchid flower is different in several ways. The ovary comes below the floral parts and appears to be part of the pedicel, so that it is hardly distinguishable from the rest of the flower-stalk unless fertilisation takes place, when it swells up into a very obvious seed-pod. The sepals, of which there are three, are in nearly all cases as attractive and brightly coloured as the petals themselves, of which there are also three. Two of these petals are usually similar in appearance to the sepals, but the third – at any rate in the vast majority of cultivated orchids – is strikingly different. It is usually much enlarged, and greatly modified in shape. In some species it has been turned into a receptacle like a small slipper, or even a bucket, into which visiting insects fall, and from which they can only crawl out along a path that compels them to bring about cross-pollination. In most cases, however, the lip, or *labellum*, as this third petal is called, does not use such crude, physical methods to trap visitors but relies on more subtle (though equally effective) devices, such as frills, markings, furry surfaces and raised lines, to entice the visitor into the centre of the flower, where it is likely to find a *spur*, containing nectar, at the end of its journey.

In most of the orchids popular in cultivation another remarkable modification has taken place. So as to provide a convenient and comfortable landing-place for pollinating insects, the lip needs to be at the bottom of the flower. But while still in the bud stage the lip is the topmost floral segment. How can its position be reversed before the flower opens? The answer is that, by a process termed *resupination*, the pedicel is twisted completely round through 180 degrees, so that the top of the flower becomes the bottom and the bottom becomes the top. So to add to their other peculiarities most orchid flowers are upside-down.

A profound difference between orchids and other flowers, including those belonging to such nearly related monocotyledon families as the lilies and the irises, is to be found in the sexual apparatus. Instead of having separate male and female organs, the typical orchid has the stamens and style completely joined together in a single structure called the *column*.

In most orchids there is a single anther at the end of the column, protected by a lid called the *anther-cap* (except for the group of slipper orchids, where the column bears two stamens behind a shield-shaped *staminode*). Under the anther-cap the pollen is to be found: it is formed into waxy masses, called *pollinia*, which may number from two to eight, according to the species. There may be a stalk or strap (the *caudicle* or *stipe*), by which the pollinia are attached to a sticky gland called the *viscidium*, whose function it is to glue the whole assembly, termed the *pollinarium*, to any suitable caller, which then carries it to the next flower to be visited.

Also to be found on the column is the stigma, usually forming a small hollow on the underside, below the male parts. Into that hollow the visitor deposits the pollinarium from the previous flower. A dual-purpose sticky liquid secreted by the stigma first removes the packet of pollen from the visitor and then provides the necessary sugar to start the pollen-tubes into growth.

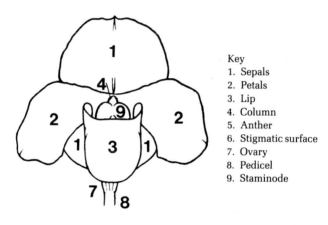

Key
1. Sepals
2. Petals
3. Lip
4. Column
5. Anther
6. Stigmatic surface
7. Ovary
8. Pedicel
9. Staminode

Typical examples of the orchid flower with (above) two anthers and (below) one anther. Note: anthers (2) are behind the staminode in upper drawing.

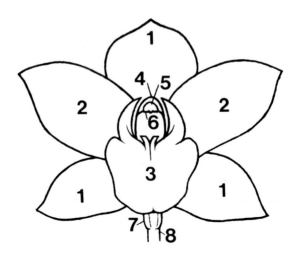

The foregoing brief description of the orchid flower is necessarily somewhat simplified; if you want to go into the subject more deeply you will find some recommended further reading at the end of this handbook. There is, however, one other structure that must be dealt with if the strange and remarkable life of an orchid is to be understood, and this is the fruit.

Phalaenopsis Lipperosa, one of the moth orchids suitable for the hot house

THE ORCHID FRUIT AND SEEDS

The fruit of the orchid, referred to by growers as a pod and known botanically as a *capsule*, may not seem of great importance to any one but a specialist breeder; indeed, the ordinary amateur who grows orchids simply for pleasure is usually at pains to see that no seed-pods are allowed to form. But the nature of the fruit, and not only the peculiarity but the sheer quantity of its contents, explain a key factor in the life of orchids; their absolute dependence upon an intimate association with a fungus during their early stages of growth, a dependence which with some species continues for the whole of their lives.

One pod of some kinds of orchid may contain nearly four million seeds, as fine as face-powder and light enough to be carried thousands of miles by air currents. Such minute seeds do not contain the store of food provided by those of most other flowering plants to enable the tiny embryo to germinate and grow. What has to happen to make up for this lack of ready nourishment is for a seed, by lucky chance, to come in contact with a fungus of the right kind and form a relationship with it. Such a relation is known as *symbiotic* – which means a 'living together' arrangement from which each partner benefits – and is quite different from a *parasitic* relationship, in which one partner exploits and harms the other.

We now know that the benefits the two partners get from their symbiotic association – termed *mycorrhizal*, from the Greek for 'fungus-root' – are that the fungus provides the developing plant with food and the plant provides the fungus with a home. Of particular importance in the diet of the young orchid are sugars, quickly absorbed and high in energy value, and the fungus has the ability to manufacture these, along with other nutrients, by breaking down more complex substances.

START IN LIFE, NATURAL AND ARTIFICIAL

Until recent years the only way to raise orchids from seed was to attempt to reproduce natural conditions by sowing on the surface of the compost in pots where orchids were already growing, so that the necessary fungus was present to infect the seed. Some people still use this method, but the results are haphazard and there are far more failures than successes.

The modern method is to raise the seedlings as 'test-tube babies', by sowing in flasks containing a nutrient jelly, which supplies the sugar and other foods that in nature are produced by the fungus. Also techniques known as 'meristem culture' have been developed, in which a tiny piece of tissue from the growing tip of a plant is cut out and grown in a nutrient soup, to produce thousands of identical replicas of the original, termed 'mericlones'. These mass-production methods have made first-class plants available at a modest price and brought what used to be a rich man's hobby within the reach of ordinary people.

In addition, the propagation of endangered species by the same methods is enabling them to be saved from extinction.

Inevitably, these artificial techniques demand specialised equipment, controlled conditions, careful sterilisation and scrupulous attention to hygiene, in order to avoid contamination. The necessary technology is beyond the scope of this handbook, and readers who wish to go into the subject more deeply are advised to consult more specialised works.

A form of *Dendrobium nobile*, one of the most widely available and inexpensive species

How orchids grow

For practical purposes, orchids are usually divided into two categories: *terrestrial*, i.e. living on the ground, and *epiphytic* (or in a few cases *lithophytic*), i.e. living on trees (or rocks). The distinction is to some extent a false one; nature is not always so black-and-white: not only are some species more correctly described as semi-terrestrial, because they are neither completely earth-bound nor completely tree-bound, but members of the same genus, and even individuals of the same species, can be found growing in different conditions.

TERRESTRIAL ORCHIDS

These include all the species native to the British Isles and other temperate zones, where in order to survive the cold they die down to the ground each autumn and spend the winter protected by their covering of soil against the killing effects of severe frost. In the spring growth starts again from storage organs underground. Some, such as the bird's-nest orchid and the coralroot, are saphrophytes throughout their lives, relying not on green leaves for their growth but on food provided by the action of mycorrhizal fungi on decaying matter in the soil. Most, however, have green leaves and are able to support themselves by photosynthesis in the usual way; but there is evidence that even they still continue to enjoy a mycorrhizal relationship; they typically inhabit woodlands, where the accumulation of decaying leaves provides ideal conditions for fungal growth, and hence for them.

Some of the most popular and widely cultivated orchids from warmer parts of the world are also terrestrial, particularly the slipper orchids belonging to the genus *Paphiopedilum*, closely related to the British native lady's-slipper, *Cypripedium calceolus*, but unlike members of that genus evergreen, since paphiopedilums do not in their native lands have to shed their leaves to face the cold.

Cymbidiums, perhaps the most popular of all orchids among amateur growers, are classified in many books as terrestrial, but in fact many of the species are epiphytic, or even lithophytic, and neither they nor the vast number of hybrids that have been raised would be likely to succeed in the sort of soil-based composts that are commonly used for the truly terrestrial orchids.

EPIPHYTES AND LITHOPHYTES

A great many of the most popular and beautiful orchids to be grown in the greenhouses of amateurs and professionals throughout the country come within this category. Some will put up with, or even prefer, cooler conditions than others, but none could be called hardy. Large numbers of them come from tropical and subtropical forests, where competition between plants for light is intense and where starting life up a tall tree or a towering rock can give a plant a head start on others that have to struggle their way up from the gloom of the jungle floor below.

Orchids of this kind have developed a remarkable type of root, able to cling tightly to the supporting tree or rock and also to take in food. Besides these clingers, many plants put out aerial roots, which may reach remarkable lengths as they hang down, absorbing moisture from the steamy air by means of a covering of silvery-looking tissue called *velamen*.

Two different types of growth are found among epiphytic orchids: *sympodial* and *monopodial*.

SYMPODIAL GROWTH

This term is used to describe the way in which many kinds of orchid, such as cattleyas and odontoglossums, develop in a particular pattern season after season. Along a connecting rhizome, a new growth appears which develops into a storage organ called a *pseudobulb* (though orchid-growers often refer to it simply as a bulb), formed from swollen stem tissue. The following season a similar growth starts from a dormant bud (or 'eye') at the base, and develops into another pseudobulb, either close beside the first or spaced from it along the rhizome, according to the species; and

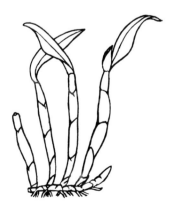

Sympodial growth, found in some epiphytic orchids.

19

so the plant progresses forward each year. If the plant is growing well, the current season's pseudobulb will be bigger than – or at least as big as – the previous year's. If the plant is not growing well, the new pseudobulb will be smaller than its predecessor – which is why when orchids are being judged at a show increase in size gains points and decrease loses them.

Each pseudobulb has a limited expectation of life, though it may last for several seasons, but the plant itself seems to be able to go on indefinitely; some sympodial orchids in botanic gardens such as Kew are known to be a century old or more and are still growing vigorously.

The inflorescences of sympodial orchids are of several different types, and may appear from the top, base or side of the pseudo-bulb, according to species.

MONOPODIAL GROWTH

Orchids of monopodial habit have a stem which grows upwards in what is termed an *indeterminate* manner; that is to say, it can go on elongating indefinitely, getting taller and taller, as new leaves and stem are formed at the apex. Among the monopodials are some of the most spectacular and beautiful kinds, such as *Vanda*, *Angraecum* and *Phalaenopsis*. Typically they come from the warmer parts of the world, and the continual upward climb enables them to push their way towards the light through lush and heavy jungle foliage.

In most cases monopodial orchids bear their flowers in inflorescences, often long and arching with many waxy blooms, from axillary points on the stem. Leaves, too, are often thick and waxy in texture, to protect them, like the flowers, from glaring sun.

Monopodial growth, found in some epiphytic orchids.

Adventitious roots appear from the nodes of the stem, and often reach a very considerable length. When the plant is growing strongly, the ends of the roots are bright green and able to photosynthesise as well as leaves; when the plant is resting, the root tips become completely covered with silvery velamen to protect them from parching heat and excessive light. Experienced growers are able to tell from the appearance of the root tips what stage of growth has been reached, and to modify the treatment given to the plant accordingly.

THE INFLORESCENCE

In the previous chapter the essential characteristics of the individual flower were explored in some detail. In this chapter on how orchids grow, it only remains to describe the way in which the individual flowers are arranged on the inflorescence.

This can consist of one solitary flower held on a single stem, as in many popular slipper orchids. At the other end of the scale it can take the form of a many-branched panicle bearing hundreds of flowers, as in many species of the genus *Oncidium*. Some of the most widely grown orchids of all, belonging to the genus *Cymbidium* and produced by the million for the cut-flower trade, carry their blooms, up to twenty or more in number, along a stem

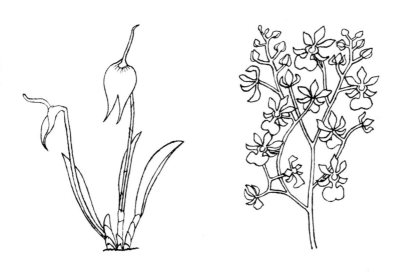

Typical inflorescences.
Left: simple (e.g. *Masdevallia*). Right: compound (e.g. *Oncidium*).

Cymbidium 'Flame hawk', a fine hybrid showing the multiple blooms typical of the genus

or main axis. Since each flower is on a short stalk, such an inflorescence should correctly be called a *raceme*, but it is universally known to orchid growers as a 'spike' (a term botanically reserved for those cases where individual flowers are unstalked, such as plantains).

In fact, you will soon find that orchid growers talking among themselves tend to call every inflorescence a spike, no matter how unspikelike. Furthermore, they have coined the phrase 'in spike' to signify any plant that has begun to develop a visible inflorescence which as not yet come into flower. Needless to say, an orchid plant advertised as 'in spike' is likely to cost you more than one that cannot be so described.

The cultivation of orchids

As you will have gathered from the necessarily brief and somewhat simplified account of what orchids are and how they grow, they are peculiar not only in their characteristics but in their habits and requirements. To grow them successfully it is important to know what those requirements are.

CHOOSING YOUR FIRST PLANTS

Few, if any, enthusiasts start by putting up a special orchid house from which all other kinds of plant are excluded. What usually happens is that someone with a small greenhouse containing a mixed assortment of different things falls for the beauty of an orchid at a show and decides it would be nice to try growing one or two. With some hesitation he asks the price. If the display has been put on by an orchid society, he is probably told that the plant which has caught his eye belongs to a member and is not for sale. If the display has been staged by a commercial orchid grower the enquirer may be in for a shock. Occasionally, if the plant is very rare and valuable, the shock will be an unpleasant one. More often the enquirer will be agreeably surprised to find that the price is very much less than all the stories about orchids being only for millionaires had led him to expect. In any case, more and more orchid nurseries nowadays clearly label every plant with a price.

Explain to the nurseryman that you are a beginner, and tell him what your greenhouse is like, what other things you grow, and what temperature your heating system is able to provide. (If your greenhouse is unheated, you will never be able to achieve satisfactory results with any of the usual cultivated orchids, but you may like to try some of the hardy and half-hardy ones dealt with on pages 51–54). The nurseryman will then be able to recommend a suitable plant or two.

Take his advice. He has nothing to gain and everything to lose by selling you something beyond your capabilities and resources, because he knows that you will only be disappointed, and may be put off orchids for ever. He wants you to be pleased with your purchase, and to feel so proud of yourself for getting it to grow and flower that you will want to try more. In short, he wants you to get hooked. He knows that once you have experienced the thrill of success with orchids you will very likely lose interest in more humdrum kinds of plants and start getting rid of them to make room for more orchids.

If you start your orchid-growing venture by joining an orchid society – which is a most sensible thing to do, since for a modest annual subscription you are able to share the knowledge and experience of other enthusiasts – you will soon find yourself offered surplus plants and propagations from other members' collections. Orchid growers tend to be generous people; once again, explain your position as a novice, and only accept plants within your capabilities and facilities.

Should a beginner start with species or hybrids? On the whole, hybrids are safer. Species are the products of natural forces, and their true home is in the wild; modern hybrids, on the other hand, are the products of human effort, and their true home is in the greenhouse. With species, therefore, an attempt must be made to create conditions sufficiently similar to those of their natural environment as to deceive them into accepting that they are at home. With hybrids, however, no deceit is necessary; they have been bred and raised artificially, and their native conditions are artificial ones.

Most likely the beginner will want (after taking expert advice on whether it is suitable) to buy a plant in flower, so that he can be sure that its colour and form are to his liking. The flowers, however, should be cut off with little delay; if in good condition they may last for several weeks in water in a vase, whereas if left on for long they will put an additional strain on a plant already having to cope with new surroundings and a new owner.

There is much to be said for buying a plant 'in spike', since without having to wait very long you will be able to enjoy the pleasure of watching the buds unfold to reveal the beauty of the flowers at their freshest.

Unflowered seedlings can usually be obtained remarkably cheaply,and offer most exciting possibilities; when they come into bloom in two or three years' time, you may find that you have an award winner which outclasses anything that has gone before. Finally, to take the guesswork (though also some of the excitement) out of buying unflowered plants,and to be assured of top quality blooms of exhibition standard, you can buy mericlones (see page 17) of awarded plants.

GREENHOUSES

As has been said, the beginner will probably start with an orchid or two in an existing greenhouse with other occupants. However, as his interest in orchids increases he may well want to make modifications; indeed, he may begin to wish he had started with a different set-up in the first place. It is therefore worthwhile considering briefly what would make the best greenhouse for orchids if one were starting from scratch.

Size

The upper limits must be dictated largely by expense, both in building the structure and in keeping it heated. The lower limit is, however, dictated by other factors. Though there are always exceptions, and some amateurs achieve miracles in houses where there is hardly room to turn round, there is a limit below which it is dangerous to go. A small structure is subject to wild variations in temperature, quickly becoming like an oven in summer and just as quickly like an ice-house in winter, should the heating system fail even for a short time. The minimum size that can safely be recommended is 8 ft wide by 12 ft long (2.4 x 3.6m), and there are many ready-made greenhouses of these dimensions on sale, framed in wood or metal. Whichever kind you choose, it is a good idea to buy one for which the maker provides extra sections to add to the length in case you decide to extend the house in the future. Some people prefer a square house, say 10 ft by 10 ft (3 x 3m), because it conserves heat better and also allows for some centre staging as well as the two lengths of staging along the sides; you will not, however, find square houses so readily available 'off the peg'.

Construction

Though the older type of orchid house often had solid walls right up to the eaves, with only the roof glazed, opinion nowadays favours more light, so the modern house usually has glazed sides as well, down the level of the staging. Some growers advocate glazing right down to the ground, at least for certain orchids such as cymbidiums, and this has given excellent results in large commercial structures. With small houses suitable for amateurs, however, glass to ground is not normally considered suitable, the main disadvantage being the high loss of heat, and hence the high heating bills. Solid sides up to staging level are generally best, the materials most commonly used being wood, brick and concrete or breeze blocks. Both the type of material and its thickness influence the amount of heat conduction between the inside of the house and the outside. For a more detailed consideration of the thermal factors involved, consult the information and figures given in the Wisley Handbook, The Small Greenhouse.

25

Glazing

Glass is undoubtedly the best material to use at present. It is stable and long-lasting, and only deteriorates slowly, if at all. Other materials are being developed and experimented with; one day they may supersede glass (and so make cracks and breakages things of the past), but for the present they cannot compete in terms of durability and/or efficiency and/or expense. However, with the high thermal conductivity of glass and the ever-increasing cost of heating, many sensible people are now going in for double-glazing. If well done, this can save nearly half the heat loss, and so reduce fuel costs dramatically. The ideal eventually might be factory-sealed double sheets of glass, manufactured in conditions of perfect dryness, so that there is no trapped water-vapour and hence no condensation. For the time being, though, probably the most practical and economical method for the amateur is to line the greenhouse with polythene sheeting, stretched smoothly and tightly about 2 inches (5cm) away from the glass.

Floor

Except for the pathway this should be of plain earth, which is kept constantly damp, so that it helps to maintain the humid atmosphere which orchids need. In the earth beneath the staging it is a good idea to plant out leafy begonias, Tradescantia, Zebrina, ferns and other things that enjoy shady and moist conditions, both for the pleasure of their company and for their contribution to keeping the air damp.

Staging

Most successful amateur growers favour the open slatted type of staging, which has the great advantage that it allows air to circulate freely around the plants and so helps to prevent them from remaining wet too long between waterings. Some equally successful growers prefer to have solid staging made of asbestos sheeting or galvanised corrugated iron, covered with a layer of pea shingle, grit, ashes or sand, which is kept constantly damp so as to maintain a humid micro-climate around the plants in their pots. The possible danger here is that drainage may not be rapid enough or complete enough if the pots are standing in wet material; this danger can be averted, however, by placing them on top of other pots stood upside-down on the damp shingle or sand.

Site and aspect

The ideal site for an orchid house is one that is open enough to get plenty of light but at the same time sheltered from harsh winds, which if nothing is done to check them can force down the temperature inside the house even more severely than a sharp frost. Perhaps the best way to combine the maximum light with the maximum shelter is to have the house near enough to a wind-break of trees, tall shrubs or a hedge to reduce air-speed but far enough away to avoid shadows. Since the plants need all the light they can get during the gloomy days of winter, the general consensus of opinion is that the ridge of the greenhouse should run north and south.

TEMPERATURE

The most useful and practical way to give your orchids the temperature they need is to divide them into three groups: cool-house, intermediate and hot-house. (Some will grow with no artificial heat at all, in a cold house suitable for many alpine plants; these are dealt with in the chapter on hardy and half-hardy orchids, pages 51 to 54.)

COOL HOUSE

This section should have a minimum night temperature in the winter of 48° to 50°C (9° to 10°C), though in very cold weather an occasional drop to 43°F (6°C) will do no harm so long as the compost in which the plants are growing, and for that matter the atmosphere inside the greenhouse, are kept on the dry side. It is the combination of cold and damp that causes damage. Most cool-house species (or the parents in the case of hybrids) are natives of mountainous regions – or, if at lower altitudes, temperate zones – where there is plenty of fresh air, often with a decided nip in it. Their response to a cold spell is to slow down their vital processes and take a rest till things get warmer; at such a time they deeply resent wet conditions, which are more conducive to rotting than to resting.

A surprisingly large and varied assortment of highly rewarding orchids can be grown in a cool house; indeed, with the steeply rising cost of heating these days, many amateurs grow nothing but cool-house kinds. Of course, cymbidiums are undoubtedly the most popular; in every way they are the ideal orchids to start a collection with: they give a magnificent show for very little effort, and they put up patiently and tolerantly with a beginner's lack of experience.

Other suitable subjects for the cool house can be found among the genera *Brassia, Coelogyne, Dendrobium, Laelia, Maxillaria, Odontoglossum, Oncidium, Paphiopedilum* and many more.

With orchids suitable for cool conditions, the problem is often not so much keeping the temperature inside the house up during the winter as keeping it down during the summer. On a sunny day a small greenhouse can heat up very rapidly, to a point where plants begin to suffer. Many people – especially those who have to be away all day – cope with the problem by putting at least some of their orchids outside during hot weather. For those left inside, a certain amount of ventilation at night, even if it is only a crack, will bring a much needed period of refreshing coolness after a sweltering day. It is very important that there should be a marked drop in temperature at night; without it, many cool-growing orchids will not flower.

A cool house will normally not need any artificial heat during the summer; the warmth generated by the sun during the day can generally be relied upon not to fall below 50°F (10°C) at the lowest during the night. Since seasons vary considerably, it is impossible to fix hard and fast dates when the heating system should be turned on and off each year. Usually you will find that artificial heating needs to be started around the end of September and continued till mid-May.

INTERMEDIATE HOUSE

If you are lucky enough to be able to afford both the space and the extra heating costs, an intermediate house – which can be simply a section divided off from the rest by some form of partition – will greatly extend the range of orchids you can grow. In particular, you will be able to add to your collection the magnificent cattleyas and their allies, whose richly frilled and heavily perfumed flowers represent for many people the very essence of the luxury and opulence that the word orchid conveys. Also you will be able to grow a wider selection of paphiopedilums, some exquisite hybrids within the *Odontoglossum* group, and many others, including the eye-catching miltonias, commonly called 'pansy orchids'.

The minimum night temperature to which the intermediate house can safely be allowed to fall during the winter is about 55°F (13°C); the winter day temperature ought for good results to rise to at least 60°F (16°C) and preferably more. In summer the minimum night temperature should be 60°F (16°C) and during the day, with sun heat to help, temperatures of between 70° and 80°F (21° and 27°C) will be reached, if not more.

To maintain the necessary minimum temperatures, the intermediate house will not only need more heat than the cool house but will need it for a longer period of the year, starting quite early in the autumn and finishing in late spring or early summer.

HOT HOUSE

This is still often called stove-house (or just the stove), because in the old days it was where the stove used to be. Some people these days call it the warm house, perhaps in the vain hope that by giving it a less extravagant-sounding name they will somehow keep down the heating bills. Call it what you like, however, it still needs to be kept at a minimum night temperature, winter and summer alike, of at least 60°F (16°C) and preferably 65°F (18°C), or even more. Day temperature in the winter should not be below 70°F (21°C), and in the summer ought to be between 75° and 85°F (24° to 29°C). To achieve temperatures of this order, which in cold weather may involve differences of as much as 45° to 50°F (25° to 28°C) between the inside and the outside, requires a powerful heating system. It also means that even after a really hot day the temperature in the house is likely to drop below the necessary minimum at night unless it is given an artificial boost. So the heating system has to be run all, or nearly all, the year round.

Besides the high cost of keeping the hot house at the right temperature, there are other problems. Prolonged artificial heat causes the house to dry out quickly, so humidity has constantly to be increased by spraying and damping down frequently; otherwise the plants can rapidly become dehydrated, and even cooked. Ventilation is much trickier to manage with the hot house than with the cooler sections, both because at high temperatures the much-needed humidity can vanish through the ventilators in a matter of minutes, and because what can be a longed-for breath of fresh air in the cool house may be a murderous draught to hot-house plants, whose ancestral home in the jungle rarely if ever experiences anything chillier than a warm breeze.

There is no doubt that a hot-house enables its possessor to grow some of the most beautiful and exciting of all orchids: the summer and autumn-flowering vandas with their heavily textured blooms; the lovely moth orchids of the genus *Phalaenopsis*, with their graceful arching sprays of waxen flowers; the heat-loving lowland dendrobiums and their hybrids, with long spires of intensely coloured blooms in shades of rose, purple and magenta; astonishing angraecums, such as *A. sesquipedale* from Madagascar, with ivory white flowers bearing spurs 12 inches (30cm) long to accommodate an outsize moth's tongue; and many more spectacular and desirable species and hybrids. The illustration in this handbook of a selection of these warm-growing orchids will give some idea of the vast range of colour and form that they offer. However, the orchid-lover who has graduated, or is thinking of graduating, to the hot-house kinds has progressed beyond the scope of this handbook and should consult more advanced works, such as those listed on page 64.

Thermometers are very useful; indeed they are essential if you intend to take your plants and their requirements seriously. If you have separate sections you will need a thermometer for each. Choose the type that shows maximum and minimum temperatures, so that you will know how hot the house became while you were away during the day, and how cold while you were asleep during the night.

Temperature gradients. Though the classification into cool house, intermediate house and hot house is useful – indeed essential – to enable us to grow the right orchids in the right places, it fails (like most other attempts at classification) to correspond to real life. One reason is that many orchids stubbornly refuse to fit neatly into any fixed category – which is why, to the bewilderment of novices, the same species will be found under different headings in different books and catalogues.

Another reason is that within the same greenhouse conditions can vary to a considerable degree. Even at the same level there will be differences to be taken into account; plants near the door, for example, will need to be more tolerant of disturbance than those at the other end. But a much more important factor is the difference in temperature at different levels. Since hot air rises and cold air falls, the temperature in the top part of an ordinary small greenhouse may be 6° or 7°F (3° or 4°C) above that at ground level. In a larger structure with a higher roof the difference could be as much as 10°F (between 5° and 6°C) or more. It is therefore possible to grow some intermediate-house orchids high up in the cool house, and some hot-house kinds high up in the intermediate house.

One way to manage this is to have two tiers: the usual staging at a height of about 2½ ft (75cm) for the 'normal' inhabitants, and extra shelving higher up for those that like more warmth. Some heat-lovers with a climbing habit, and hence a reluctance to sit still in a pot, can be fixed to slabs of bark and hung on hooks from wires stretched along the roof.

Since generally speaking the cooler-growing orchids originate in regions of high altitude, and the hotter-growing ones come from the lowlands, what you have to do in the greenhouse is to turn the natural order of things upside-down: you put the high-altitude kinds low down, where it is cooler, and the low-altitude kinds high up, where it is warmer.

There are two possible difficulties arising from the placing of plants high up in the house. Because they are so close to the glass they will get much more light than those growing lower down, and that could be damaging to those with thin or soft leaves, not made to withstand glare and prone to scorching. More difficult still, the higher temperatures in the upper part of the house mean lower relative humidity, so plants growing there are liable to dry out very quickly and may shrivel unless they are watered much more often than would be needed if they were at a lower level; and, of course, the higher up they are the more difficult they are to water.

With skill and experience, and with the right choice of plants, some orchids will revel in such apparently unpromising conditions, especially towards the end of the summer and in early autumn when the season's growth needs thorough ripening. However, the experience needed for success takes a little time to acquire. The beginner is advised to stick to simple, straight-forward orchids which grow contentedly in pots on the ordinary staging before he feels he has learned enough to be able to move into the higher realms.

HEATING METHODS

A great deal has been written and spoken about the relative merits of different types of heating for orchid houses, and the rest of these pages could be taken up with a repetition of the arguments. However, the whole subject has been dealt with in a practical, succinct and lucid way in the publication already mentioned, the Wisley Handbook, *The Small Greenhouse*, which compares, in terms of BTU (British Thermal Units), the output, the efficiency and the economy of various sources of heat. Briefly, these sources include electricity, gas, oil and solid fuel. You will notice that these have been put in alphabetical order. By coincidence, that also represents the order of convenience, starting with the most and ending with the least convenient. And, because convenience is something that has to be paid for, it also happens to represent roughly the order of running costs, starting with the most expensive.

Electricity is often referred to (particularly by those who sell electricity or electrical appliances) as a high-grade source of heat, meaning that all you have to do is to switch it on; you avoid the chores of refuelling, stoking and cleaning. Many people, especially those who are away much of the day, are happy to pay the extra unit costs of electricity to be rid of such chores. There is the added advantage that control by a thermostat will save unnecessary heating on a sunny day and will switch on auto-matically again when the temperature falls. The most commonly used electrical devices are tubular bars and fan-heaters. Many of the latter have built-in thermostats, and these can be quite efficient; but for maximum accuracy a rod-type thermostat is best. Fan-heaters are preferred by many because they circulate the air round the greenhouse (some types, indeed, can be set to blow air even when the heating element is off), but they should be so placed that they do not aim hot air directly at any plants.

Electrical immersion heaters can also be used in hot water systems, as described later (page 33).

Gas can, if properly used, be an efficient, convenient and reasonably economical form of heating. There is still some prejudice against it, dating from the days when gas mains dis-pensed a poisonous mixture, the combustion of which released fumes which could have a lethal effect on plants. The natural gas of the present day, however, is non-poisonous, and the burning of it simply adds moisture and carbon dioxide to the air. Water vapour is just what orchids need, especially to counteract the otherwise drying effects of artificial heat. As for carbon dioxide, it is used as a growth stimulant in commercial glasshouses, where heaters are often on all day during the active growing season (though it can hardly be expected to have the same stimulant effect in the usual amateur's greenhouse in winter, when growth is minimal, or even at a standstill). Besides the gas heaters that run off the mains, there are now models that use bottled gas. Whichever type is used, thermostatic control should be included, to save fuel and money.

Oil is probably the most widely used method of heating for small greenhouses at the present time. A blue-flame paraffin heater can be bought very inexpensively at any hardware store and most garden centres, and will give excellent results if correctly placed and properly looked after. It must not be stood under staging or plants – both because its flame might be damaging to them and because it would most likely be extinguished by a deluge every time watering took place – so it must, in a small greenhouse, be found a place on or just beside the path, and care will be needed to see that it does not get in the way. It is absolutely vital that the wick should be trimmed with the utmost care and regularity, so as to make sure that it does not smoke or give off noxious fumes; plants tend to be more sensitive than human beings to that sort of thing, and fumes undetectable to the nostrils can cause promising flower-buds to drop off, or even worse things to happen. Since the burner needs a good supply of oxygen to keep alight, it is most important that the greenhouse is not too airtight, or the heater will go out; if necessary, a small sliding vent in the door should be enough.

Many oil-heaters have a water-tray on top which is filled up regularly and adds a little useful humidity to the atmosphere.

It goes without saying that the tank must never be allowed to become empty, but most heaters nowadays have a fuel gauge.

Solid fuel was the usual source of heating for a very long time; all the great orchid collections of the past relied on boilers burning coal, anthracite or coke and circulating hot water through a system of cast-iron pipes. They also relied on old-fashioned cheap labour to carry out the task of stoking, cleaning out and ash disposal, as much as three or four times a day. More efficient boilers have been developed, fed automatically, but even these need attention at least once a day.

There is a lot to be said for hot-water systems; they give a very even, constant heat without awkward hot-spots or cold-spots. However, most people nowadays would probably decide against the use of solid fuel because (a) of the drudgery involved, (b) a substantial, covered fuel store is needed, and (c) supplies may be uncertain, and you run the risk of finding yourself down to your last shovelful on the coldest day of the year. The alternative of a boiler fired by gas or oil has a great deal to recommend it; control can be entirely automatic, and apart from regular servicing there is little or no maintenance needed. Finally, you can heat your water system with an electric immersion heater; this has the advantage of costing considerably less to instal, but running it can be extremely expensive if its kilowatt rating is high enough to do the job properly.

Large-scale modern installations tend to use small-bore piping, 2 inches (5cm) in diameter, because experts have proved that its proportionately larger surface area gives out more heat. However, an electric pump must be installed in order to force the water round. The amateur is better advised to go in for the traditional 4 inch (10cm) flow and return pipes, in which the water circulates by convection currents, with no need for a pump. There is the added advantage that the greater volume of water in the larger pipe will stay hot much longer in the event of a breakdown.

HUMIDITY

Of all the factors that go into good orchid cultivation, this is perhaps the most important. As we have seen, orchids differ from all other plants in the structure of their flowers. They also differ from almost all other plants in the way they grow, and particularly in their water requirements. To provide them with the conditions they need in the greenhouse, you must *water the air*. Because of the peculiar nature of their structure, especially of their roots, they demand a relative atmospheric humidity of between 75 and 85% for good growth – a considerably higher level than would be healthy for many other greenhouse plants such as pelargoniums. (For comparison, the British climate gives an average relative humidity reading of around 55 to 60% on a fine day, but the figure can go well below this on a hot, dry day.)

Damping down is the time-honoured and effective way of maintaining the high humidity required. The process consists of spraying plenty of water over the paths and earth and on the staging between the pots containing the plants. Damping down should be done early in the morning nearly every day of the year, except perhaps in the cool house on a cold morning when the air seems already moist enough; but remember that a cold, wet day outside does not necessarily mean a damp atmosphere inside: indeed, if the heating system has been going full blast things may be drier than usual and call for more, not less, damping down.

As the day wears on, the sprayed water will be drawn up into the air to give the required humidity. When the weather becomes warmer it will be necessary to give a further damping down towards evening, to replenish the atmospheric moisture that has dried out during the day. During the summer another damping down may be needed in the middle of the day, and extra ones still when the weather becomes really hot. Tap water should be used for damping down; rainwater is too precious for the purpose, and should be kept for watering the plants, which may react unfavourably to substances often present in water from the mains.

Though it is sometimes said that certain orchids from steaming jungles and tropical rain-forests cannot be cultivated successfully except in a hot-house atmosphere so saturated that a drip forms on the end of your nose almost as soon as you go in, most cool-house and intermediate-house orchids do best in an atmosphere that, though moist, is comfortable for people. As you become more experienced, you will soon learn to judge whether the humidity is right or not. Till then, it is a good idea to buy a hygrometer and hang it up among the plants; chose one with a clearly marked dial, on which a needle, controlled by the expansion or contraction of a hair according to the dampness of the air, gives a precise reading of the relative humidity (a measure of the percentage of moisture in the air in relation to the temperature, hot air being able to hold much more water vapour than cold air can).

In addition to the damping down of floor and staging, plants greatly appreciate an overhead spraying with rainwater in a fine mist during warm summer days. Make sure, however, that you do the spraying early enough for it to have dried off by nightfall; water left on plants when the sun – and the temperature – goes down is likely to lead to rotting.

Oncidium concolor, an epiphytic orchid which may be grown in the cool house

LIGHT

Recent advances in knowledge have shown that in the past orchid growers tended to give their plants too little light. Heavy shading was applied to the glass, and the resulting gloom made it difficult for leaves to perform their function of photosynthesis fully, or for growths to ripen properly; and without ripening there is little chance of high-quality flowers – or even of flowers at all.

There are, it is true, some orchids that belong naturally to shady places, such as gullies or the floor of the jungle, where what light manages to reach that far has been filtered through the canopy of leaves above. The most important cultivated orchids of this type are the paphiopedilums, which therefore need special shady conditions (see below). New growths, even of the sun-loving kinds, may need protection from undue glare in their early stages, before they are tough enough to face full light.

However, most shading of greenhouses has been, and is still, carried out in order to protect plants against excessive heat rather than too much light. On a sunny day the temperature inside a small house may quickly become dangerously high. In such conditions dehydration may occur, giving rise to severe damage from leaf-scorch. If the danger can be averted by keeping the air moist and by creating an artificial breeze (a small electric fan will do this admirably), then plenty of light can be a positive help to firm, healthy growth. All the same, some form of shading will be necessary for most greenhouses at certain times; a plant that has had too little light can survive, and may be restored to health and vigour if the deprivation is only temporary, but a plant that has been fried is finished.

SHADING

The ideal method of shading is by means of a blind outside the roof of the house and held a little above it, so that the sun's rays will already have been broken and subdued by the time they hit the glass. For many years the best material for the blind was considered to be slats of wood, fixed flexibly together so that they could be rolled up and down, or sideways along the roof, according to the state of the light. (There were arguments about whether the slats should run horizontally or vertically; on the whole the vertical arrangement won from the theoretical point of view, and the horizontal arrangement won from the practical point of view.) These slatted blinds can still give excellent results, but latterly there has been a trend towards the use of plastic mesh, which being lighter is more easily controlled (especially by modern automatic methods using photo-electric cells).

The great advantage of roller blinds is that they need be used only on sunny days. In duller weather they are rolled back so that the plants can benefit from full light. However, they are not cheap to instal and – unless fully automatic – they need attention. Many amateurs therefore use the cheaper and easier method of brushing or spraying a coat of greenhouse shading mixed with water on to the glass; as it dries it becomes semi-opaque and reduces penetration by the sun's rays considerably. It is usually applied in the spring, when a sudden burst of sunshine can spell danger for new growths, and kept on till late summer, when – if it has not already been washed away by heavy rain – it is removed with a wet cloth or sponge. Green shading is widely used, but many experienced growers prefer a white version, both because there is less colour distortion to the light it transmits and because when wet with rain during dull weather it becomes more transparent, and so lets through more light.

VENTILATION

Most orchids – particularly of the cool-house types that the amateur is likely to begin with – welcome plenty of fresh air. But they are apt to resent draughts, and may show their aversion to icy blasts by dropping their flower-buds, by arrested growth, by proneness to disease, or even by sudden death. For that reason ventilators at staging level, through which air from outside directly impinges on the plants, would never be used (better still, they should never be installed).

Box ventilators with sliding doors, let into the wall under the staging – on both sides, so that one or other can be opened or closed according to the direction of the wind – and preferably covered inside the greenhouse with fine-mesh plastic or gauze to keep out bees and other insect nuisances, are excellent. The air admitted through them, regulated by the width to which they are opened, will be at the correct greenhouse temperature by the time it reaches the plants. Many successful growers leave one or more of these box ventilators open, at least slightly, all the time – except perhaps in extremely hostile weather.

Roof ventilators must be used with the greatest caution. Since hot air rises, it may be thought that the quickest and simplest way to cool things down if the atmosphere becomes overheated is to open the top ventilators wide and let it all out. True, but along with it would go the precious humidity, and within a very short time the air inside the house could be bone dry. Thorough damping down and spraying before the ventilator is opened might help, but even then it would be rash to open too wide. A chink of top ventilation is usually much safer.

Electric fans can be of enormous help in keeping the air on the move while avoiding draughts and preserving humidity. Small ones may be bought quite cheaply and since they use very little current their running costs are low.

COMPOSTS

Of all the many changes in methods of cultivating orchids during the last decade or so, probably the most profound have been in the materials used as ingredients for composts. That is why any book on orchid-growing published more than some fourteen or fifteen years ago is likely to be hopelessly out of date.

The revolution in potting methods came about largely because the traditional osmunda fibre, the wiry roots of a fern imported mainly from Japan, had become exceedingly expensive, so that substitutes had to be sought.

Most modern orchid composts are based on bark (usually pine or fir) and/or peat, with the addition of inert material such as sharp sand, grit, Perlag or Perlite (both made by heat treatment of volcanic rock to produce a light and porous substance) to keep the mixture open and provide good drainage. Some use shredded or broken plastic, such as polypropylene or expanded polystyrene, for the same purpose. Many add fragmented dried leaves and/or chopped sphagnum moss, with perhaps a little broken charcoal to keep the mixture sweet. A serviceable compost for most epiphytic and semi-terrestrial orchids is as follows:

3 parts medium grade bark (dust-free)
1 part granular peat
1 part Perlag or Perlite (or $1\frac{1}{2}$ parts coarse grit)
  to which may be added, if available
1 part chopped sphagnum
1 part broken dried leaves and 1 part charcoal.

Many orchid nurseries have their own formula. Some add a pinch of bonemeal to the mix when potting; others do not. Everything depends upon what suits their growing conditions. Mixing different composts together can do considerable harm. The best thing a beginner can do is to go to a reputable orchid dealer and ask for plants that will go on growing happily in the same pot for two or three seasons before they need repotting. Then he will have gained experience in how to manage them by the time the operation becomes necessary.

An amateur's greenhouse containing a mixed collection of orchids

REPOTTING

There are two reasons for repotting: (a) that the compost has deteriorated and needs replacing, or (b) that the plant has outgrown its present pot and needs a bigger one. In the first case the existing compost must be discarded, together with any rotten or unhealthy roots, which should be cut cleanly away. In the second case there is no reason why such compost as remains clinging to the roots should not be left on them, instead of being torn off, with consequent damage, so long as both compost and roots are in good condition (dead or unhealthy roots are usually shrivelled and brown, while healthy ones are plump and white).

The bottom quarter of the pot is filled with coarse, inert material to ensure perfect drainage; in the old days broken pieces of clay pot ('crocks') were used, but nowadays people use all kinds of things, from lumps of expanded polystyrene to stones and pebbles (which have the advantage of weighing the pot down and so making it less easy to knock over). All that is then needed is to hold the plant at the correct height in the pot and pour the compost round it; a smart tap or two on the bench will be enough to settle the compost round the roots.

WATERING

Of all aspects of orchid-growing, this probably more than any other determines success or failure. The beginner, used to dealing with the demands of most other greenhouse plants such as fuchsias or tomatoes, has become accustomed to the idea that if anything is allowed to become dry at the roots it will suffer badly and very likely die. He finds it hard to believe that there are plants which not only put up with the almost complete drying out of their compost between waterings but actually depend on such treatment for their well-being. Yet that is precisely what nearly all cultivated orchids need.

In natural conditions they are subjected to torrential downpours during the rainy season, but in between these they rapidly dry out. What we must do is to create similar conditions in the greenhouse. When water is needed, a thorough soaking should be given; after that the compost should be allowed to become nearly – but not quite – dry till the next time. People new to orchid-growing are often totally confused when they hear or read the much-repeated injunction not to water too much, and think it means that only a trickle of water should be given. Far from it. When you water do so generously; the injunction not to water too much simply means not to water too often. Compost that is constantly sodden will cause roots to rot; and the affected plant, because it is no longer able to take up water, will show just the same symptoms as if it had been kept too dry: yellowing, shrivelling, and – if it is not quickly rescued – death.

The question most frequently asked by novices is 'How often should I water?' The only honest answer is that there is no answer, because conditions vary so much. Once every two or three days may be necessary in the height of summer, and once every two or three weeks in the depth of winter. The requirements of each plant must be judged individually; neighbours on the staging may have very different needs. After a time you will be able to judge at a glance; till then you may find it useful to lift the pots and compare their weight: the heavy ones probably do not need water, while the light ones probably do.

If possible, it is best to use rainwater, preferably from a tank inside the greenhouse, so that it is at the right temperature. The watering-can should have a long spout, so that the water can be directed exactly where it is needed, instead of being splashed about in all the wrong places.

Plants hung up on slabs of bark or in baskets cannot be watered in the same way as those in pots; they are usually dealt with by dipping them in the water-tank for a few minutes till air stops bubbling from them. Be sure when you hang them up again that they do not drip on plants below them, which may cause severe damage.

Watering should always be done in the morning – ideally a sunny one, when the temperature is rising. Then there will be time for the surface of the compost to dry off by the evening, a particularly important precaution during the winter.

Finally, there is one little rhyme about when and when not to water which, if obeyed, should save a lot of grief, both to plants and to those who grow them: *If in doubt, leave it out.*

RESTING

Up to this point we have dwelt mainly with ways of helping orchids to grow. That is, however, by no means the whole story. There comes a time in their life-cycle when what they want to do is not to grow but to rest; and if we are to be successful with them, especially in getting them to flower, we must help them through that period as well. The reason why orchids have pseudobulbs and other storage organs is much the same as the reason why camels have humps: to tide them over unfavourable conditions. These include drought, cold, and any other set of circumstances which makes growth difficult or impossible – even the shedding of its leaves by a deciduous tree on which an epiphyte is growing, thereby robbing the orchid of shade and exposing it to unbroken glare.

During its resting period an orchid needs little or no water. Unfortunately it is impossible to give general rules which apply to every type, because the length of rest varies widely, from a week or two in some cases to several months in others. The only true guides are experience, observation and expert advice (though experts do not always agree). It is, however, possible to say that those orchids that lose their leaves completely during the winter should have their watering reduced as the foliage turns yellow in the autumn and should be given no water at all – or only just enough to prevent excessive shrivelling – during their leafless resting phase; watering can be cautiously started again when they show visible signs of growth. Those that retain their leaves, and hence are more liable to loss of moisture even when at rest, will probably require a little more water.

FEEDING

Feeding of orchids was once frowned upon by most growers, but modern composts do not provide much nourishment in themselves, so a feed has to be given from time to time during the growing season. Liquid fertilizers are the most convenient, since they can be added during watering. There are special mixtures for orchids, but one of the general-purpose liquid feeds should be perfectly satisfactory. Many experienced growers produce prize-winning blooms by giving a high-nitrogen feed at the beginning of the season to stimulate growth, and a high-potash one (a tomato fertilizer is admirable for the purpose) later on to encourage flowering.

Orchids are not gluttons, so when using a general-purpose fertilizer it is wise to play safe and dilute it to half the recommended strength. It is also wise, at any rate until you have gained experience, not to feed too frequently; once in every three waterings during the growing season should be enough to begin with, dropping to once in five or six (if at all) during the winter.

PROPAGATION

Methods of propagation can only be dealt with very briefly in this elementary handbook. Simply to grow orchids successfully takes knowledge and practice. To propagate them successfully takes a good deal more of both.

Raising orchids from seed is a laboratory operation needing special equipment and precise scientific control. Propagation by vegetative means (i.e. by division) is all that concerns us here. The operation is performed in one of two ways, which may be described as major and minor surgery. (A third method already referred to in passing, meristem or tissue culture, is another laboratory technique beyond the scope of this handbook.)

Keiki (otherwise spelt *ki-ki*, but not to be found in the dictionary in either form) is a word orchid-growers use among themselves to mean a small plantlet which appears on a pseudobulb or stem, and which if left for a while usually sends out roots into the air. Remove such plantlets – preferably with a sharp knife, to avoid tearing – and plant them into small pots containing compost, which should be rather loose so that the young roots can get plenty of air. Water very cautiously at first, but spray the leaves with a fine mist, till the roots have adjusted to their new conditions.

Cuttings from mature plants to form new propagating material can be made in several different ways, and may call for major surgery. Side branches of monopodials such as vandas can be sliced off and potted separately when their roots have grown about 3 in. (7 to 8cm) long. Leggy, top-heavy specimens may have the top removed, with its attached aerial roots, and planted separately; in time, if all goes well, the remaining bottom stem will develop new side branches.

Sympodial orchids with pseudobulbs, such as cymbidiums, cattleyas and odontoglossums, are divided by cutting through the rhizome connecting the pseudobulbs – sometimes a tough job, calling for strength, determination and a sharp knife. When an orchid of this kind has reached the edge of the pot in its forward growth it will need repotting anyway, and the back part of the rhizome, together with the old pseudobulbs (which have probably lost their leaves by now, and are contributing nothing to growth), is cut away, so that the newer part can be placed with its back edge against the rim of a fresh pot, leaving room in front for it to grow forward for a few more years before it reaches the edge and needs repotting again.

Instead of being discarded, the old 'back-bulbs', as they are called, can in suitable circumstances be coaxed into producing new growths from dormant buds ('eyes') at the base; where there is an exposed rhizome, as with cattleyas and their relations, many people cut half way through it with a V-shaped nick in late summer, to encourage the dormant eye to plump up, and new roots to form beneath it, before the rhizome is completely severed in the following spring. Incidentally, all division should normally be carried out in spring, when warmth is returning, days are lengthening, vigorous growth is beginning, and healing of cuts is rapid.

Various other methods are used to propagate new plants from divisions and cuttings, and can be learned by experience, by further reading and by advice from fellow orchid-growers. One final point needs to be added: do not carve up plants aimlessly. Propagations may take years to reach flowering size, by which time the original plant, if left intact and potted on as required into larger receptacles, might have grown into a magnificent specimen, festooned with flowers and carrying off prizes at shows.

The most popular orchids

Since there are probably at least 25,000 natural species of orchid, plus some 60,000 artificial hybrids, choosing which ones to deal with and which to leave out would be a massive task if this were a large volume aiming at anything like a complete treatment of such a vast and complex family. In a small handbook written for the novice it is only possible to give a tiny selection. Those dealt with in this chapter have been chosen because they are (a) easy to grow, (b) inexpensive, (c) readily available, and (d) beautiful. They also include a large number of excellent hybrids, which, as already pointed out, are ideal for the beginner because a greenhouse is their natural environment.

CYMBIDIUMS

These are probably the easiest of all cool-house orchids to grow, and they give spectacular results for very little effort. The genus *Cymbidium* (named from the Greek *kymbe*, boat, because of the shape of the lip) has about 50 species, coming from India, the Far East – including China and Japan – and Australia. Few of these species are in cultivation, most growers preferring the superb modern hybrids. They have egg-shaped pseudobulbs, sheathed by the bases of the long, narrow leaves. They flower mostly in spring, often producing twenty or more blooms to a stem, which is usually tall and stately. They come in a variety of brilliant colours – green, white, yellow, red, in fact almost everything but blue – and are extremely long-lasting; it is not unusual for them to remain in perfect condition for two or three months before they begin to fade. (However, it is better for the plant's well-being to cut the flowering stem after three weeks or so; it will probably last another five or six in a vase of water.)

Many different composts can be used successfully for cymbidiums, provided that, while sufficiently retentive of moisture, they are free-draining enough to allow plenty of air to reach the thick, fleshy roots. The mixture given on p. 38 suits them well. Some growers, using large containers, have achieved splendid results with a half-and-half mixture of peat and gravel.

With regular feeding during the growing season, cymbidiums can make very large plants, and that may create problems for people with small greenhouses. Fortunately during the past few years the situation has been eased by the breeding of many beautiful miniatures, resulting from crosses with small species such as *C. pumilum, tigrinum, ensifolium* and *devonianum*. From these first-generation miniatures further crosses have been made, producing hybrids with larger flowers on plants still neat and compact enough to fit comfortably into a small house.

PAPHIOPEDILUMS

Many orchid-fanciers consider these to be the true aristocrats of the family; some, indeed, grow nothing else.

The genus *Paphiopedilum* (derived from words meaning Venus's slipper) consists of some sixty species, native to a wide area stretching from India and Burma to the Far East. Though they all share the popular name 'slipper orchids', because of the pouched lip resembling a small slipper, they vary considerably in their habits and requirements, as might be expected of such a large number coming from so many different habitats.

Most old books on orchids will tell you that slipper orchids (which they will almost certainly call by the erroneous name *Cypripedium*, correctly applied only to those from colder climates which die down during the winter) are of two kinds: plain green-leaved ones that can be grown cool, and mottled-leaved ones that need more heat. Things may once have been as simple as that, but many of the modern hybrids are of such mixed parentage that the distinction has become somewhat blurred. It is true that the easy-going *Paphiopedilum insigne* (the type species on which the genus is founded), coming from the Himalayas, will put up with coolish conditions. Most species and hybrids are safer and grow better in intermediate temperatures.

Though specialists in slipper orchids tend to have their own composts, the mixture given on page 38 will give perfectly good results. Since paphiopedilums have no pseudobulbs or similar storage organs, the compost must never be allowed to get too dry; on the other hand it must not become soggy or the roots will rot. Paphiopedilums need a considerable amount of shade and should not be exposed to direct sunlight. However, shade does not have to mean the depths of gloom; leaves require a reasonable amount of light to do their work properly.

CATTLEYAS

The sumptuous flowers of cattleyas and their relations, usually with intricately frilled or fringed lips and often heavily scented, are what the word orchid conjures up in the minds of many

people. They are felt to represent wealth, luxury and sophistication, which is why they tend to be the orchids pictured in glossy
magazines and on expensive boxes of chocolates, to convey a
sense of glamour and justify the price.

The genus *Cattleya* (named by the great botanist John Lindley to
honour the eminent orchid-grower William Cattley) comprises
some thirty species of epiphytes – occasionally lithophytes –
native to central and south America. In addition, there are several
other related genera, all from parts of America or the West Indies,
which can readily be crossed with cattleyas and with each other.
There are now dozens of artificially created new generic combinations within the group, many of very mixed parentage
involving not just two but three, four or even five different genera.
These combinations may lead to some complex and cumbersome
names (see page 63). They can also result in some large, striking
and somewhat unreal-looking flowers, which those who like them
call showy and those who are not so keen call overpowering, or
even vulgar.

Most cattleyas do well in the intermediate house. With their
tree-dwelling origins, they need a very free-draining compost; the
mixture on page 38 should suit them, though some growers, in
order to speed up the drainage, might prefer to reduce or
eliminate the sphagnum and/or add a little more Perlag, Perlite or
grit.

All cattleyas rest during the winter, and during that time need
little or no watering. They will tell you when to prepare to water
again in the spring by the swelling of a bud at the base of last
season's pseudobulb, which will develop into a vigorous shoot
and start to send out roots. Water gently at first; they will be reluc-
tant to enter wet compost; some roots indeed may grow across the
surface and hang down over the rim: do not cut these or damage
their delicate growing tips, but spray them with water to keep
them plump and healthy.

Cattleyas can do with plenty of light, to help them to grow well
and to ripen the developing pseudobulbs in order to promote
flowering. This happens in rather an odd manner. As growth
nears completion, what looks at first like a new leaf appears; this
is the sheath, through which the flower buds will push their way
when blossom time comes.

Opposite: *Paphiopedilum* hybrids (left) do best in the intermediate
house; *Odontoglossum* hybrids (right) will succeed in cooler conditions
Opposite below: the sumptuous large flowers of *Sophrolaeliocattleya*
Jewel Box 'Dark Waters' are characteristic of this epiphytic genus

ODONTOGLOSSUMS

Members of this group are considered by many to be at once the most graceful and the most beautiful of all orchids. With their long, arching sprays of delicately sculptured and often intricately patterned flowers, they are highly decorative, whether in the greenhouse or arranged in a vase or made up into an elegant corsage.

The genus *Odontoglossum* (from the Greek words for tooth and tongue, because of the projections on the lip) consists of about a hundred species of epiphytic or lithophytic orchids native to tropical and sub-tropical central and south America, and mainly confined to the mountainous regions. Like those other popular American orchids the cattleyas and their relations, odontoglossums form part of a large tribe (Oncidieae), which contains many other genera, one of which – *Oncidium* – has four times as many species as *Odontoglossum* itself. These genera can be crossed freely with each other, and as a result there are now nearly as many artificially created intergeneric hybrids in the group as there are among the cattleyas and their relatives. The pleasing thing is that so far the breeders have not produced in the Odontoglossum group anything that could be described as overblown or vulgar; the offspring of even the most complex crosses manage to retain a sort of innocent charm.

Because of their origins in regions of high altitude, nearly all the species and hybrids in the Odontoglossum group will do well in quite cool conditions, though some of the hybrids – at any rate the modern ones – are more accommodating in this respect. However, the temperature in the winter should not be allowed to drop much below 50°F (10°C) at night, and then only if the plants are rather dry – but not bone-dry – at the root; it is the combination of cold and wet that is the real root-killer. The standard compost mixture given on page 38 should suit the plants well, but it must never be allowed to get soggy, especially when the weather is cold.

With the spring, new growths will start to push, and they should be encouraged to grow vigorously by increasing the temperature a few degrees. Damping down should be attended to so that the atmosphere does not lose moisture because of the extra heat. New roots must not be allowed to shrivel through dryness; on the other hand, they are extremely liable to rot in their early stages if they remain wet. Allow the compost to dry out between waterings, but not for more than a day or two.

Summer is really the most trying time for odontoglossums. Like some people, they become difficult during hot weather; the maximum that most of them can stand is about 85°F (29°C), but they prefer something lower. Every effort should therefore be made on sunny summer days to keep things as cool as possible, by shading, by ventilation, by frequent damping down, by spraying, and by watering: in hot weather it is sometimes right where odontoglossums are concerned to forget the wise maxim 'When in doubt, leave it out' and change temporarily to 'When in doubt, water it'.

DENDROBIUMS

It is impossible in this handbook to deal more than very briefly with these orchids, since they belong to the second largest genus in the family. Most of them are of little or no interest to the amateur, but a few bear flowers of great charm and beauty.

The genus *Dendrobium* (from Greek words meaning tree-living, because most species grow on trees) has probably 1,000 species – it is impossible to be more precise, both because botanists argue over the figure and because new species keep being discovered. They are nearly all epiphytes, with a few lithophytes, and they originate from a very wide area, India eastwards to China, south-east Asia, Japan, and south through the Pacific Islands and Papua New Guinea to Australia and New Zealand.

Many of the species are quite easily grown by experienced orchidists; other are fiendishly difficult. The most popular and widely cultivated dendrobiums, however, are the selected forms and hybrids. These fall mainly into two groups: those usually referred to as *Dendrobium phalaenopsis* types (though many other species may have gone into their make-up), and those deriving from *Dendrobium nobile* and other members of its section. The first kind produces those spires of glowing flowers with a brocade-like texture which you sometimes see in a high-class florist's window; magnificent though they are, they need a lot of heat to grow them well and so will not be dealt with further here. The second kind thrives in cooler conditions and is very suitable for a beginner; there are many cultivars to choose from, and they make a fine sight when in flower.

The needs of these *nobile* types are plenty of warmth and humidity during their rather short growing season and a cool, dry rest afterwards. During the winter it is essential that the tempera-ture should not be allowed to rise too high; 50°F (10°C) is quite enough, and some successful growers prefer 45°F (7°C), at least for a period, to provide the shock considered necessary to get them into flowering condition. Buds will start to swell at nodes along the 'cane', as the elongated pseudobulb is called, quite early

49

in the year, and it is from these buds that the flowers will develop some weeks later. It is taken as a sign of skill if the cane can be induced to flower from as many nodes as possible, right down towards the base. If temperatures were allowed to rise too high during the winter you will probably be disappointed, because those promising buds are likely to produce not flowers but little plantlets.

When new growth starts in the spring it should be encouraged to develop as rapidly as possible, for which purpose many growers move the plant from the cool to the intermediate house. Water the compost (the standard mixture on page 38 will do well) at first with care, but make sure it really is wetted; after its dry spell in the winter the water may run straight through it, so repeat the dose once or twice at the first watering. As growth increases, give the plant plenty of light, to keep the new cane vigorous and firm, and to help it to ripen. When growth is completed in the autumn – shown by the production of a single smallish leaf at the end of the cane – you should start reducing the watering, and stop for the season by winter, when the plant will be ready again for its cool rest.

SPECIES

As you become more proficient and confident, you may decide to try some species in addition to your growing collection of hybrids. It provides interest and something of a challenge to study their varied habits of growth and try to reproduce something resembling the conditions in their native habitat. Many of the species are of modest size and can be fitted in among the larger kinds without overcrowding. Some do best if hung up on pieces of bark or in wooden baskets. Your widening circle of orchid-growing friends will press upon you small propagations from their own treasured plants. If you go to orchid shows and meetings, you may win the odd plant in one of the raffles they usually hold on such occasions. Pretty soon you may find yourself wondering about having another orchid house.

Hardy and half-hardy orchids

A question very often asked is 'Are there any hardy orchids, and if so can I grow them in my garden?'

The answer to the first part of the question is 'Yes, certainly'. The answer to the second part is 'Maybe, but probably not'.

As already explained, there is hardly a corner of the world without some native orchids. In the British Isles alone no fewer than fifty-three species, plus another ten or more sub-species and varieties, have been found growing wild. Why then is 'Can I grow them in my garden?', given such a discouraging answer?

First, these hardy terrestrial orchids are quite unlike the cultivated kinds we have dealt with up to now. They die right down to the ground after flowering, and instead of aerial pseudobulbs (which would instantly rot in the soil) they rely for survival on underground storage organs in the form of fleshy rootstocks and tubers. They are not adapted to the cultural conditions and the air-filled composts, designed mainly for epiphytes, that we have so far considered.

On the other hand, these hardy terrestrials will not put up with ordinary garden conditions either. Their natural habitats are almost entirely woodlands, which cater in several ways for their very special requirements: (a) the branches overhead protect against the most extreme cold, which is at its worst when there is nothing interposed between the earth and the sky; (b) the layer of fallen leaves both enriches and lightens the soil and provides perfect conditions for the growth of mycorrhizal fungi on which the life cycle of the plants depends.

Lacking the same advantages in the open garden, the hardy terrestrials turn out to be not so hardy after all, nor as well provided for nutritionally. Some people manage to keep a few species alive in pockets of specially mixed soil, with plenty of leafmould and grit, in the rock garden, but not often for long. Most of them are really much safer and better off in an unheated alpine house, where on the coldest days – and even more on the coldest nights – they will enjoy conditions nearer to those in their woodland home than they would if they were out in the garden. You will also be able to grow a wider range of such orchids in an alpine house, including some from more southerly temperate climates, often called – sometimes for convenience rather than accuracy – Mediterranean species.

One point must be made here with the greatest possible emphasis. Because of recent, long overdue legislation designed to protect endangered species of plant from extinction, it is now illegal to collect these temperate-zone orchids from the wild. However, with modern laboratory methods of propagation a stock of plants is being built up, and some are now obtainable from a few specialists, though at present in very limited quantities. Among the species you may find available are several charming slipper orchids (*Cypripedium*) and members of many other genera, such as *Coeloglossum*, *Epipactis*, *Gymnadenia*, *Himantoglossum*, *Ophrys*, *Orchis* and *Spiranthes*, with such evocative common names as Frog, Lizard, Bee, Fly, Spider and Butterfly Orchids, Scented, Musk and Spotted Orchids, Helleborine and Lady's-tresses.

When you receive your purchases the rhizomes or tubers will be dormant. They may be planted in a mixture of one part each of fibrous loam, sharp sand or grit, and crumbly leafmould which has been well sieved. To prevent rotting, plant no more than an inch or so deep and stand the tuber on a little extra sand. When planting is finished, cover the surface with a layer of sand, or better still grit, so that when the leaves appear they will not be resting on damp soil. A light spraying with water after planting should be all that is needed till early autumn, when the pots should be stood outside to catch the rain. Before the frosts start, bring them under glass; give good ventilation but do not expose them to really hard frosts. Growth will begin in spring, first the basal leaves and then the flowers. When these have faded, cut them off to avoid weakening the plant. Reduce watering as the leaves start to yellow and die down, and then let the pots dry out during the rest of the year.

In addition to the mainly European orchids dealt with so far in this chapter, there are two genera of attractive hardy or near-hardy orchids from the Far East which are readily available, easy to grow, and very rewarding when they come into flower.

BLETILLA

The genus *Bletilla* (named from a fancied resemblance of the flowers to those of the American genus *Bletia*) consists of some nine species native to east Asia. The only species commonly to be found in cultivation is *Bletilla striata*, which comes from Tibet, China and Japan, and with good cultivation can grow up to 20 in. (50cm) tall, with a graceful inflorescence carrying several rose-pink flowers with deeper markings on the lip; there is also a white-flowered form. This is among the most attractive of the hardy terrestrial orchids and may be grown out of doors, but for safety's sake it should perhaps be protected from really hard frosts. It gives excellent results in the cold house, where it may be grown in the compost mixture suggested above, with the tubers planted about 2 inches (5cm) deep.

PLEIONES

These are considered by many to be the most beautiful of all the orchids that can be grown successfully in cold conditions. Though they are sometimes described in books and catalogues as hardy terrestrial orchids, and indeed are dealt with as such for judging purposes by the RHS, they are neither truly terrestrial nor truly hardy.

The genus *Pleione* (in Greek mythology the mother of the Pleiades, who were transformed into a cluster of stars by Zeus in a fit of pique) is generally considered by botanists at present – with a few arguments – to consist of nine species, native to mountainous regions in the Himalayas and in parts of China and Indochina. There are, however, many different cultivated varieties, the majority of them named cultivars of *Pleione formosana* (once considered to come within the species *P. bulbocodioides*), such as 'Clare,' 'Lilac Beauty', 'Oriental Splendour' and 'Snow White'.

Bletilla striata, delicate in appearance but hardy and undemanding

'Oriental Splendour', a popular cultivar of *Pleione formosana*

In the past few years, as growers have turned more and more to orchids that require little or no heat, interest in pleiones has increased and several beautiful hybrids have been bred. We may expect many more, as the number of *Pleione* addicts increases.

In the wild, these orchids do not grow in soil but in shallow patches of debris at the base of trees, on fallen logs and on rocks. For successful cultivation they need to be given the same conditions: a shallow root-run (best achieved by growing them in pans rather than pots, and putting plenty of drainage material at the bottom) and a very open compost: the standard one on page 38 gives good results. The pseudobulbs – leafless in the winter and lasting only one year – should be half-buried in the compost. When new growth begins in the spring, watering can be started, but be very cautious at first because the young roots are easily rotted. The flowers appear either just before or at the same time as the new leaves start to unfold, and last a week or two before starting to fade. Watering should be increased in accordance with the state of growth; when leaves begin to fade and wither during the autumn, watering should be decreased; after leaf fall and through the winter the pseudobulbs should be kept dry (but not so dry as to make them shrivel).

If growth has been vigorous, two or three plump new pseudobulbs will have formed during the season, and these can be split up and replanted separately; the old bulb will have shrivelled and should be discarded.

Growing orchids indoors

All orchid growers who have the well-being of their plants in mind will cut off the flower-spike from long-blooming kinds after two or three weeks in order to conserve the plant's energy. The flowers will then be brought indoors and stood in a vase of water, where they will decorate the house for several weeks more.

With those kinds that do not produce spikes of flowers suitable for this kind of treatment, the grower has often brought the whole plant into the house, to enjoy the blooms in the living room and perhaps to show them off to visitors. He has, however, usually taken them back into the greenhouse quite soon, so as to restore them to more congenial surroundings, knowing that if he attempted to establish indoors the humid conditions they require he would most likely cause the human occupants to suffer discomfort and the furniture to grow mould.

Now that the cost of fuel has risen so high, many orchid growers and would-be orchid growers have started to wonder whether ways could be found to grow the plants indoors without causing problems for the other inhabitants, human and otherwise. Since the rooms are being heated for the residents anyway, could not the same heat be used for growing orchids without any extra cost?

Some success has already been achieved, by such means as growing the plants on a suitable window-sill, each pot being placed on another pot, inverted and stood on a tray of pebbles, kept constantly wet so as to produce a micro-climate of humid air around the plants by evaporation. The window should admit plenty of light, but the direct rays of the sun may cause leaf-scorch to some plants, especially thin leaved ones or those with young growths at a vulnerable stage. One way to tackle the problem is to have the plants on a table a little way from the window; but be careful not to place this too far inside; light intensity can fall off steeply as one moves farther into the room. An excellent idea is to put the plants on a trolley – a tea-trolley will do admirably – which can be moved back from the window when the sunlight is too strong. To refresh the plants and prevent them from becoming too dry, spray the leaves with water from time to time. Do not use the ordinary type of garden spray, or you will get splashes all over everything and make yourself very unpopular. Use an 'atomiser' type, which can be bought very cheaply and delivers tiny droplets in a fine mist; not only will it do no damage but it might noticeably improve the atmosphere – which in a modern house, especially a centrally-heated one, can become a bit too dry even for human beings.

Among the orchids that can be grown in this way are cymbidiums (miniature ones preferably; standard kinds are apt to grow too big), some of the paphiopedilums, laelias, dendrobiums of the *nobile* type and many oncidiums.

The best method of growing orchids indoors is to have them in some sort of glass case, where they can enjoy a suitably humid atmosphere all to themselves. The old-fashioned Wardian case, made of leaded panes of glass surmounted by a domed or pointed cover and used in Victorian times for growing ferns and other things that thrive in moist air, is coming back into its own, and specimens that would have been turned down even by a junk-dealer a few years ago now change hands at fancy prices. The modern equivalent, called a plantarium and looking rather like a fish-tank, might not be so elegant, but it does not cost a fortune and it can give very good results indeed.

More sophisticated, and giving much wider scope for growing, are the new types of cabinet now appearing on the market. Some of them amount to fully equipped small greenhouses for indoor use; and some manufacturers will make you a special custom-built one to fit a recess, an alcove or a bay window. There is every imaginable optional extra: automatic humidifying and watering, thermostatic temperature control and fluorescent lighting, to give your plants ideal growing conditions. With such equipment the only limits to what you can grow are the size of the cabinet, the temperature, and other conditions, that you can afford to maintain inside it.

The striking *Oncidium bifolium* 'Patrick', which received an Award of Merit at Chelsea in 1986

Pests and diseases

The subject of pests and diseases has been left almost till the end of this handbook for two reasons. First, it would be a pity to discourage the beginner by dwelling on the calamities that might, but almost certainly never will, befall his plants. Second, very few pests and diseases attack orchids anyway. Such troubles as they suffer from in cultivation are much more likely to be the result of faulty management than of outside agencies.

The most important thing to stress is that scrupulous attention should be paid to hygiene at all times. Unfortunately there are many people who would not dream of jeopardising the health of their family by leaving decaying rubbish around in the home but who do not seem to mind jeopardising the health of their plants by leaving a squalid mess in their greenhouses. A golden rule is to remove all dead or decaying matter as soon as you see it. It is also a good idea to get into the habit of keeping not only weeds but garden plants away from a strip 3 or 4 ft wide (90–120cm) all round the greenhouse, and so deny pests and diseases the hosts they need in order to feed and breed before making their way inside. (It is, of course, unthinkable that you will allow weeds inside the greenhouse itself.)

If you buy your orchids from a reputable firm you can be pretty sure that they will be clean and healthy when you receive them; apart from a proper pride in professional standards, no dealer would be so foolish as to endanger his stock and his reputation by any slackness. Gifts from friends are another matter. No matter what you have been taught about never looking a gift horse in the mouth, examine any plant you have been given, or won in a raffle at an orchid society meeting, with great care. If it shows signs of infestation or infection, treat the conditions thoroughly before admitting it to the company of your other plants; some people spray, or fumigate, or even dunk such acquisitions, pot and all, in a bucket of pesticide, as a routine safety measure, no matter how clean and healthy they look. Orchids can sometimes be damaged by pesticides if they are not used with care. Avoid spraying plants which are exposed to bright sunlight or extremes of temperature. Seedlings and open blooms are more sensitive than mature leaves and they should not be sprayed unless absolutely necessary. Plants with ensheathing leaves should be laid on their sides after treatment in order to drain off excess spray.

Since in spite of strict precautions troubles may occur, let us now take a brief look at possible culprits and how to deal with them.

PESTS

Aphids (greenfly) do not very often attack the plants themselves, but they do sometimes go for the flowers and spoil them. Fumigation or a quick spray with pirimicarb, derris or malathion will soon dispose of them.

Mealybugs and *Scale insects* are sometimes a nuisance, fastening themselves to pseudobulbs, stems and the undersides of leaves, sucking out the sap and weakening the plant. Keep a look out for them when you go round watering, and if you find any deal with them immediately. If there are only a few, they can be dealt with in an old-fashioned but still effective way by painting them individually with a small brush dipped in methylated spirit. Spraying with malathion or systemic insecticide will be necessary for larger infestations (though they should never have been allowed to occur).

Red spider mites (which are more likely to be pale yellow than red) can, if they get a hold, do much damage to some of the softer-leaved orchids by breeding – at a horrifying rate – on the underside of the foliage and sucking the sap. Since they are so minute that they can only be identified under a magnifying glass, often the first sign of their presence is a yellowish speckling of the leaves. The assertion is persistently repeated that they cannot survive in conditions of adequate humidity. That is nonsense; there seem to be some strains that are thoroughly at home in wet conditions. (It should be added, though, that the plants suffer more in dry conditions, because then the loss of precious sap is more damaging.) When established – especially when they have settled in and covered themselves with a protective web – they can be difficult to eradicate. Sprays containing derris, dimethoate or malathion are used against them, and it is a good plan to ring the changes, to avoid building up a resistant strain of the pests. Once they are under control it is a wise precaution to give a routine spray against them once a month or so, as many commercial growers do. Greenhouse aerosols can also be used to discourage the mites.

Slugs and *snails* can do considerable damage by gnawing roots and young, soft leaves. What they particularly like are flowers, and they can completely ruin a promising spike's prize-winning

Scale insect and young

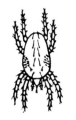

Red Spider Mite

Aphid

Mealybug

Some frequent pests of orchids, all greatly magnified

chances by one night's nibbling. Slug pellets containing met-aldehyde or methiocarb will deal with the pests, as will beer in a container on the floor, which will attract them and in which they will drown. Another method, which many find more satisfactory, is to go out with a torch at night to track them down and kill them.

DISEASES

Well-grown, robust plants are unlikely to fall prey to disease. It is usually wrong treatment that causes trouble, particularly wet compost (which may simply be because of a drip from an unnoticed crack in the glass), stagnant air (which might be remedied by an electric fan), and/or low temperature combined with high humidity. In such conditions, rot can set in with alarming speed, the symptoms being brown or black spots accompanied by softening of the plant's tissues. If the disease has not gone too far the affected part can be removed with a sharp knife, but make sure you cut right back to healthy tissue, with no sign of blackening. If the rot has gone so far that the plant has begun to collapse into a soggy mess, take it out of the house and burn it, before the infection spreads.

Many growers find it a wise precaution to dust any cut surface, even that caused by cutting a flower spike, with powdered sulphur or a proprietary fungicide. Any knife used should always be sterilised between operations by passing it through a flame or dipping it in spirit.

The most insidious complaint from which orchids can suffer is infection by virus. Hygiene can do a great deal to prevent it, since it is spread by being introduced into the plant's tissues by insect pests or by unsterilised knives or other instruments. There are various forms of virus disease, with symptoms ranging from light or dark spots to streaks and mottled patterns. The plant may become stunted and weakened, flowering poorly or not at all. It may, however, continue to live for a long time, providing a dangerous source of infection for other plants. For that reason it is best, if you can bring yourself to do so, to remove any infected plant and burn it, since there is no way of curing it.

Sophronitis coccinea, a popular miniature species from Brazil with flowers of exceptional brilliance, easily grown in the cool house

The naming of orchids

Those new to orchids are often baffled by their names. Their puzzlement is understandable, even if the names are not, because in some ways the naming of orchids is more complicated than that of any other plants.

The subject, though not a difficult one, would take far more than the space available here for an explanation of all the finer points. In any case, those wishing to go more deeply into the matter will find every aspect dealt with in full detail in the *Handbook on Orchid Nomenclature and Registration* published in 1985 by the International Orchid Commission. We will deal therefore only with a few of the more important points that a beginner would need to know so as to be able to understand what is meant by the words on a label that he might find attached to a plant in an orchid nursery or at a show.

Take as an example one of the most famous of all hybrids in the most popular cultivated orchid genus, *Cymbidium* Alexanderi 'Westonbirt' FCC/RHS. What do all those word and letters mean?

A group of *Miltonia* hybrids, known as pansy orchids and ideal for the intermediate house

As is generally known, a natural species normally has a botanical name consisting of two words in Latin, the first (the generic name) signifying the genus, and the second (the specific epithet) signifying the species within that genus. By international agreement, for the sake of uniformity in scientifically acceptable printed matter, both words are in italics, the first being given a capital and the second a small initial letter. Two species, *Cym. eburneum* and *Cym. lowianum,* were crossed together, and the resulting hybrid flowered in 1889 and was given by its breeders, the famous firm of Veitch, the name *Cym.* Eburneo-lowianum, the new coinage now being put into roman type, with a capital letter, to signify that it is not a natural species but an artificial hybrid. Some years later this hybrid was crossed with a third natural species, *Cym. insigne,* and, after some of the resulting seedlings had flowered in due course, the new hybrid was named Alexanderi, after the name of the hybridiser, H. G. Alexander. All the seedlings from that cross, no matter how dissimilar, were called Alexanderi; and what is more all the offspring of any subsequent remake of the same cross must be given that same name too. In other words, Alexanderi is in effect the surname, which all the offspring of that marriage or remarriage have in common. Nowadays we call that the grex name (from the Latin *grex,* a flock).

However, all the offspring of the same marriage are not necessarily the same. As it happened, when one particular offspring of the Alexanderi cross came into flower, it was so outstanding that it was given the additional, individual name 'Westonbirt' (now called the 'cultivar' name, short for 'cultivated variety') and put in front of the Orchid Committee of the RHS. The Committee were so impressed by its quality and beauty that they gave it a First Class Certificate (always referred to by the knowledgeable as FCC/RHS).

So that explains the sequence of words on the label: the generic name *Cymbidium* in italics; the grex name Alexanderi in roman type with a capital letter to proclaim the fact that it is an artificial hybrid; the cultivar name 'Westonbirt' in single quotation marks to show that it is the name of a single, unique individual out of the flock; and the designation FCC/RHS to signify that it received the coveted award of a First Class Certificate from the Royal Horticultural Society.

The method of naming outlined above has remained substantially the same since the naming of the grex Alexanderi in 1911, though there has been a series of modifications for the sake of logic and clarity; for instance, the hybrid name Eburneo-lowianum would no longer be permitted, since it has a scientific ring about it because of its Latin form: nowadays a grex name must be obviously a 'fancy' one – that is, it must be in such a form that nobody could possibly mistake it for a scientific botanical name.

A problem that became apparent some years ago to the RHS, as the International Authority for the Registration of Orchid Hybrids, was the remarkable extent to which orchids within certain sections could be crossed with each other, not merely within the same genus but between different genera. For instance, as mentioned on page 46, there are many genera within the Cattleya group which can be freely interbred, to create combinations of three, four, or even five different ones. At first the hybrid generic names of such crosses were coined by combining parts of the names of each genus involved. Thus, *Brassavola* crossed with *Laelia* crossed with *Cattleya* became *Brassolaeliocattleya*. To have gone on in the same way beyond that would have offended both against comprehensibility and against international agreements not to make names so long that they acted as a barrier rather than as an aid to communication. When, therefore, longer combinations were threatened, it was decided to simplify matters by making names for such new hybrid genera by adding the suffix -*ara* to the name of someone esteemed in the orchid world. So when *Brassolaeliocattleya* was crossed with *Sophronitis* the name given to the result was not *Sophrobrassolaeliocattleya* but *Potinara*, in honour of Monsieur Potin, President of the Paris Orchid Society.

As more and more interbreeding goes on, so the names of more and more eminent orchidists, plus -*ara*, are being used for new combinations.

As International Authority, the RHS only registers grex names. The suggestion is sometimes made that the register should extend to cultivar names as well. However, with registrations of grex names currently running at 175 a month, and the possibility of hundreds, or even thousands, of individual cultivars in each grex, the suggestion is hardly a practical proposition at present.

Further reading

The Complete Book of Orchid Growing, by Peter McKenzie
  Black (Ward Lock).
Growing your Own Orchids, edited by W. Ritterhausen.
  (Salamander Books).
Manual of Cultivated Orchid Species, by Bechtel/Cribb/Launert
  (Blandford Press).
Orchids in Colour, by B. & W. Ritterhausen (Blandford Press).
Orchids for Everyone, Ed. Brian Williams (Treasure Press).
Orchid Growing Illustrated, by B. & F. Ritterhausen (Blandford Press).
Orchids and How to Grow Them, by Bailes & Moon (Eric
  Yound Orchid Foundation).
Orchids as Indoor Plants, by B. & W. Ritterhausen
  (Blandford Press).
Popular Orchids, by B. & W. Ritterhausen (Burnham Nurseries).

Orchid societies

If you want to get full enjoyment and satisfaction from your orchid growing, the sensible thing is to join an orchid society, to benefit from the experience and friendship of other orchid enthusiasts. There is probably a society or a group of orchid-lovers near you who would be delighted to welcome you as a member. Most of them meet regularly, to show plants, to exchange experiences, to ask for and give advice and help, to attend talks both by members and by visiting speakers, and to enjoy outings to shows and orchid nurseries.

The national society, affiliated to the RHS, is the Orchid Society of Great Britain, with a large and growing membership throughout the country and with several local groups. It exhibits regularly at Chelsea Flower Show, where its displays of members' plants have won several gold medals over the years. It provides members with an informative journal four times a year and has a regular programme of meetings, shows, talks and outings. It also has an extensive library of books and slides which can be borrowed by members.

For full details of membership and of local groups of orchid lovers write, enclosing a stamped addressed envelope, to:

L. E. Bowen, Hon. Secretary,
The Orchid Society of Great Britain,
28 Felday Road, Lewisham, London SE13 7HJ.